Brother Roger and Taizé
A new springtime

By Fr Bryan Wells

All booklets are published thanks to the generous support of the members of the Catholic Truth Society

CATHOLIC TRUTH SOCIETY
PUBLISHERS TO THE HOLY SEE

Contents

Christianity's best kept secret	3
Roger's early years	5
Taizé and ecumenism	14
Taizé today – a new springtime	25
Visiting Taizé	26
Why come to Taizé?	33
Four secrets of Taizé	39
The Sacraments at Taizé	41
Taizé and Rome	44
A reflection	46

Christianity's best kept secret

Many people associate Taizé with a style of music or with specific songs such as "Jesus, Remember me" or "Bless the Lord my Soul". Some may have heard of Br. Roger, who started the Taizé community, or know that Taizé is a place in France, while others associate it with a contemplative spirituality. These associations are all true – but they are only glimmers of the actual community of Taizé.

Unlike most religious communities, Taizé does not have a long history – at time of writing (2012) only seventy-two years.

From his arrival at Taizé in 1940 until his death in 2005, Br. Roger's life was totally dedicated to living the way of Christ, to solidarity with the poor and to seeking the reconciliation of churches, individuals and nations. Focusing on the gospel's essence has enabled the Community to speak to the lives of millions of young people over the years.

Through the work of the brothers of Taizé, countless people have been privileged to witness one of their key qualities in action: adaptability. In developing their Community, they have consistently listened for and adapted to the call of God for their collective life. Taizé is not a scheme or a programme, but rather an evolving community which as the years have passed has sought to adapt to young people, to their needs and priorities as well as to their anxieties. The Taizé community's fundamental question (which perhaps should be fundamental for all Christians) is "how do we live out the gospel in and through our lives?"

It has sometimes been said that the social teaching of the Catholic Church is its best kept secret. In a similar way, perhaps Taizé is Christianity's best kept secret, despite the fact that millions of young people aged 17-35 have visited the hill in Burgundy since the 1960s. It is impossible to describe Taizé – it must be experienced!

The main themes to emerge from the community

- Seeking the unity of the disunited Christian church throughout the world. The community is thoroughly ecumenical and has ordained and lay members of most of the major denominations, including several Catholic priests.
- Seeking the unity of the human family – the community is international in composition
- Sharing solidarity with the poor- the community is involved in social projects in some of the most deprived areas of the world.

The church at Taizé is called the Church of Reconciliation, and this word, perhaps, best sums up the mission of the Community. For me, it is one of the most hopeful signs in human life.

Roger's early years

Roger Schutz was born in Provence, Switzerland; he was his parents' ninth and last child (a tenth did not survive.) His father, Charles Schutz, was a Swiss Protestant pastor, and his mother a French Protestant from Burgundy. His siblings included a much older brother and seven sisters. Of these, Geneviève, a gifted pianist, was to have a profound effect on Roger in his later years and was eventually an indispensable help to her brother in caring for refugees in Taizé during World War II.

Love for music

We get the impression of a solitary but not lonely boy. The house was always full of visitors, and Roger wrote that his childhood, far from being sad and lonely, was full and active. The house was full of music – pianos and a gramophone – and the young Roger developed a love for Bach and Chopin, who would often move him to tears. In later years, in the company of his Taizé brothers, he loved listening to music, "through which the plenitude of God is made more accessible."

Seeking reconciliation within

Perhaps the most significant and abiding event for Roger was the arrival, shortly after World War I, of his maternal grandmother. She had lived in the north of France during the war, but eventually moved to the Dordogne where, although a Protestant, she would regularly attend Mass in the Catholic Church and receive Communion. Probably as a result of the intense suffering she had witnessed, she seems to have been penetrated by a desire that no one should ever again go through what she had experienced. This led her to seek reconciliation of various kinds. In Europe, divided Christians were slaughtering one another: let them at least be reconciled so that another war might be prevented.

Roger wrote: "she did not seek to justify her actions or talk about it, but I understood that by going to the Catholic Church she was effecting an immediate reconciliation within herself. It was as if she knew intuitively that in the Catholic Church the Eucharist was a source of unanimity of the faith." For Roger, she was to become "a witness, a symbol of reconciliation because she reconciled within herself the strain of the Protestant and the Catholic faith."

The twin themes of sympathy for the distressed and achieving reconciliation within oneself were to have a lifelong effect on Roger.

Catholic influences

His father's influence, however, was just as long lasting. During one of the many family walks in the Swiss mountains, Charles Schutz broke off from the party to enter a Catholic church. "He remained there praying for a long time then emerged without saying anything. This influenced me profoundly... It must be because he found there something which he did not speak of but which have been very powerful."

During a stay with an uncle, Roger found himself rising early and going to Mass in the church opposite, returning somewhat embarrassed to find the family at breakfast. These Catholic influences remained with Roger and were to become one of the major building blocks of the eventual Taizé community.

Education and illness

At first, Roger was largely educated at home, supervised by his father, but aged thirteen he was sent away from home for his secondary education. He lodged with a Madam Boiley, a woman of deep Catholic faith and an acquaintance of his parents. Daily communion was the norm and with the Boiley family Roger experienced a truly joyful Catholicism and imbibed its ethos. However during this time - his teenage years - he contracted tuberculosis, possibly from one of the Boiley daughters who was to die of the disease. He was ill for several years and came close to death. The long period of his recovery, however, was also to be formative. He took long walks in the mountain air and he also studied with the idea of becoming a writer. Charles Schutz however was firmly opposed to this, and insisted that Roger read theology, and this is what, finally, he did when, in 1936, he registered to study for four years at the University of Lausanne and Strasbourg.

The Grande Communauté

During his final year, in 1939, he was asked to become president of the Protestant Students' Federation in Lausanne. Roger had always had an interest in monastic living and from this motivation was formed, under his leadership, a kind of third order called the Grande Communauté. It was made up of twenty students who, through prayer and work, attempted to help their fellow Christian students out of their isolation and towards a common purpose in life. The Grande Communauté met bimonthly for a colloquium featuring prominent Protestant intellectuals, and also retreats because, said Roger, "retreats are necessary for much converse with God and little with his creatures." These retreats consisted of meditation, examination of conscience, and confession. They attracted many people but for Roger, the Grande Communauté was a prelude to an even greater adventure and a much larger perspective.

The Second World War

The solitude, reading and long walks of Roger's late adolescence were now to bear fruit. He wrote of a "kind of instinct... a certainty that something was going to happen." A retreat made at this time in a Carthusian monastery made an indelible impression, especially the community prayer. War had broken out and Roger struggled to decide his own course of action. "I found myself as if impelled to do everything I could to find a community life in which reconciliation would be realised, more concrete day by day. To begin with I must start a life of prayer alone. I would find a house where there would be prayer in the morning, at midday and in the evening, and I would take in those who were fleeing and those in hiding."

This vision of reconciliation was not very far removed from that of his grandmother before him. Europe was being torn asunder and Roger asked the vital question "why is there such opposition and conflict between human beings and especially between Christians?"

"He had asked himself whether a way existed on the earth for one person totally to understand another and he resolved that if such a way existed, a way that meant seeking to understand everything about another rather than to be understood by them, he must commit himself to it and pursue it until death."

A Place of Prayer

France surrendered to Germany in 1940. Not only had the invasion caused terrible destruction, but Jews and other political refugees were reduced to fleeing from Nazi persecution to "unoccupied" (Vichy) France and from there to the safety of neutral Switzerland. It was these people, often penniless and starving, whom Roger felt compelled to help.

So, in August 1940, he travelled to Burgundy, where some of his mother's relatives still lived, to look for a suitable house. After several interesting possibilities, a lawyer in Cluny drew his attention to the nearby village of Taizé where a house large enough for his purposes had stood unoccupied for many years. He cycled to the village and found Taizé half abandoned and in ruins. A series of bad harvests had turned the land into a desert.

An old peasant woman showed him the house. He was hungry after his journey, and the old woman invited him to stay for a meal, at the end of which she made a poignant appeal: "Stay with us, we are so alone. Buy the house and stay here!" Roger was profoundly moved and thinking of Christ's reverence for the poor was won over. "I chose Taizé because the woman was poor. Christ speaks through the poor and it's good to listen to them. Contact with the poor prevents faith from becoming vague and unreal."

This Taizé house would now become the base for the Grande Communauté and in December 1940 it held its first meeting in what they called the house of Cluny. When the meeting ended, Roger stayed in the house, but he was seldom alone. Taizé was situated just a few miles from the border between occupied territory and Vichy France, and he was confronted with a constant stream of refugees, some more dead than alive. He took them in and cared for them but also prayed three times a day in a room converted into a chapel.

Even in these early days, a monastic ideal was forming in his mind. He wrote "every day let your work and rest be quickened by the Word of God; keep inner silence in all things and you will dwell in Christ... be filled with joy, simplicity and mercy."

This way of life continued until November 1942. While helping refugees across the Swiss border he learned that the German authorities had occupied the house in Taizé and taken the refugees prisoner – a local inhabitant had denounced him. Shaken by this blow Roger accepted the consequences and stayed in Switzerland. With Max Thurian, a theology student, and Pierre Souverain, he rented a house in Geneva close by the historic cathedral. There they were joined by a fourth man, Daniel de Montmollin, and the four young men committed themselves to temporary celibacy and community of material goods, praying each morning and evening in a side chapel of the cathedral. In 1943, Roger was ordained as a Reformed Pastor having successfully completed his doctorate on St Benedict and the monastic ideal – a subject which raised some eyebrows in Protestant circles.

Eventually the house of the four young men became a focal point for students, workers and trade union officials; their strong links with working people was to be one of the major themes of the eventual Taizé community. In fact, the preface to Roger's first book, *Introduction to Community Life* was written by a group of metal workers.

He wrote: "We are isolated from one another, and that breeds resignation. How can we make a break with our all-too-individualistic tradition? How can we make use of the immense possibilities which are liberated when people work together and live in communities?"

The rest of his life would answer that question.

Return to Taizé

Roger and his three companions returned to Taizé in 1944 and learned of the hatred of the local French population for the German prisoners of war in a camp near the village, which had resulted in the murder of a German Catholic priest. The brothers attempted reconciliation and even visited the prisoners, sharing what little food they had with them. Although some locals took offence, a profound Christian impact was made on the area. The brothers also took in twenty war orphans who were looked after by Roger's sister Geneviève.

The Taizé community was (and is) completely self supporting. In 1947, due mainly to the agricultural skills of Pierre, the surrounding land was cultivated and the community became financially stable. Hospitality was given to a whole range of people, Catholics and Protestants, who came to see these "twentieth century monks" and their daily round of prayer and work. Visitors increased, and permission was eventually given for the brothers and visitors to pray in the tiny 12th Century Romanesque church (adjacent to the present day community house.) The permission was given by the Papal Nuncio to Paris, Angelo Roncalli - the future Pope John XXIII.

The small community further expanded in 1948 when three young Frenchmen - one a doctor – joined, and so, by the start of 1949, the community numbered seven. In the spring of that year a great step forward was made when these seven took the three traditional monastic vows: lifelong celibacy, a total sharing of goods, and acceptance of authority, represented by Roger as Prior.

Thus came into being what has been called the first Protestant monastic community.

Taizé and ecumenism

From 1949, the Taizé community became a reality. One of the great goals of the community had always been ecumenism – the unity of the Christian Church, sadly divided over the centuries. Throughout the 1950s, they undertook all kinds of ecumenical initiatives, including the establishment of cordial relations with the local Catholic bishop of Autun, and also with the Vatican through the offices of Mgr. Montini - later to be Pope Paul VI

The definition of the dogma of the Assumption of the Blessed Virgin Mary in 1950 was to prove a setback, not so much because of the doctrine itself, but because it was defined infallibly. Papal infallibility had been formally defined at the first Vatican Council in 1870, and had always been a stumbling block between Catholics and the churches of the Reformation. Roger feared that the definition of the Assumption would not help inter-church relations. However, contact was maintained with Mgrs. Roncalli and Montini and good relationships developed in France between the community and the Abbé Couturier (architect of the Week of Prayer for Christian Unity) and also with the aged Archbishop of Lyon, Cardinal Gerlier. In 1950, Br. Roger first met the Pope, Pius XII.

It was not until 1953 that Br. Roger wrote out the Rule of Taizé. Like most monastic Rules (the charter of regulations governing a community) it was the fruit of experimental living. The Rule of Taizé is not prescriptive but attempts to suggest a spirit and to motivate and inspire a way of life. It is solidly based on phrases from the Scriptures. The first brothers - all Protestants - would have been well versed in Scripture.

Roger wrote: "There is a danger... in only having indicated the essentials for a common life... Better to run that risk, and not settle into complacency and routine. That Christ may grow in me, I must know my own weakness and that of my brothers. For them I will become all things to all, and even give my life for Christ's sake and the Gospels" (Rule of Taizé).

A new phase

In 1958, Angelo Roncalli was elected as Pope John XXIII and a new phase began in Taizé's relationship with the Catholic Church. Before Pope John was inaugurated,, Cardinal Gerlier of Lyon appealed to him to grant Br. Roger an audience to discuss the role of ecumenism in the Catholic Church. Only three days after his inauguration, Pope John received Br. Roger and Br. Max who were delighted with the Pope's enthusiasm for reconciliation. Each year since then the brothers have had an audience with the Pope. During his short pontificate, John XXIII grew to cherish the Taizé community and on one occasion, seeing Br. Roger approaching, he declared "Ah, Taizé, that little springtime", a statement that might be said to characterise the community even today.

The opening of the Second Vatican Council

From the early 1960s, more and more young people "invaded" the hill of Taizé. In October 1962, also, the Second Vatican Council opened, a Council which was permanently to alter the Catholic Church's relations with other churches and, indeed, with other religions and with the wider secular world.

The Community produced a text in advance of the Council, expressing its hopes and its apprehensions. It is worth quoting it here in full:

> "Recognising clearly the scandal of the separation existing between us who are all Christians, we are in quest of a visible unity. It and it alone can render possible an outburst of mission capable of bringing the glad news of the gospel to every person in the world.
>
> ...We know that the Catholic Church maintains that she has preserved intact the unity desired by Christ. It is not for us to judge that conviction. But it must be said that the manner in which that unity is affirmed is frequently hurtful to those who are not Catholic. When the Catholic Church expresses the goal of Christian unity in terms

such as 'returning to the fold' or 'submitting' to her, dialogue at once becomes impossible.

Surely, it would be possible to employ a term implying 'a common advance towards' or 'fulfilling together' total unity? Otherwise there can be no real dialogue. Protestantism needs repeated declarations of the kind made by the Pope: 'We will not put history on trial. We will not try to establish who was right and who was wrong. Responsibilities lie on both sides. All we shall say is, Let us unite! Let us put an end to disagreement!'"

This appeal bore fruit. In September 1960, and again in 1961, Br. Roger invited a dozen Catholic bishops and fifty Protestant Pastors to meet at Taizé for three days. This was one of the first gatherings of its kind since the Reformation and Br. Roger invited all participants to share their common pastoral concerns and the problems each was experiencing in the contemporary world.

The Council issued its Decree on Ecumenism (*Unitatis redintegratio*) on 21st November 1964, and its Declaration on the Relation of the Catholic Church to non-Christian religions (*Nostra Ætate*) on 28th October 1965. Henceforth ecumenical engagement was central to the mission of the Catholic Church.

The Church of Reconciliation

More and more people were coming to Taizé, and thoughts turned to building a church large enough to hold the crowds. On August 6th 1962, the Church of Reconciliation which had been built by German volunteers was opened. The opening was attended by representatives from all the major Christian denominations.

Br. Roger spoke at this inauguration drawing attention away from the building to the message that lay beyond it: "Consciously or not, those who come here are searching for something beyond themselves. When they ask for bread, how can we offer them stones? When they have been in the Church of Reconciliation, it is better for them to remember the call of reconciliation and, with this as a basis, to prepare the daily bread of their lives, rather than to return home with only the memory of stones."

The Council of Youth

By 1963, the new church was in great demand and in 1971 it became necessary to knock down the rear wall and replace it with huge doors which could be raised to allow for a marquee extension. The Seventies were indeed a decade of expansion and the insistent questions for many of the young pilgrims was "How can we take home what we have experienced here?" From this question, the Council of Youth was born in April 1974.

Public recognition and awards

That year brought public recognition for the Taizé community, including the award to Br. Roger of the Templeton Prize, an annual award given for spiritual contributions. It had been awarded to Mother Teresa in 1973. Br. Roger immediately gave the £34,000 prize money to organisations working with immigrants in the UK, to those working in the peace process in Northern Ireland, and to those helping the poor in South America. Br. Roger was also given the German Peace Prize.

The annual "Letter from Taizé"

Although Br. Roger had never wanted fame, the world had now taken notice of the Taizé community. It was also in 1974 that he started his annual "Letter from Taizé" – written to young people throughout the world to help sustain them in their "Pilgrimage of Trust" – an idea which has inspired most of the Community's international work since that time.

Mother Teresa's visit

In August 1976, Mother Teresa visited Taizé and in return Br. Roger took a group of five brothers and ten young lay people to Calcutta, to live among the poorest of the poor. For five weeks they worked, prayed and slept in poverty, working under the direction of Mother Teresa. It was out of this situation of poverty disease and despondency that Br. Roger and Mother Teresa composed this prayer:

"Oh God, the father of all
You ask every one of us to spread
Love where the poor are humiliated,
Joy where the church is brought low,
And Reconciliation where people are divided:
Father against son, mother against daughter,
Husband against wife,
Believers against those who cannot believe,
Christians against their unloved fellow Christians.
You open this for us, so the
Wounded body of Jesus Christ may be the
Leaven of community for the poor of the earth and for the whole human family."

European meeting

Throughout the 1980s, the brothers continued to live among the poor around the world. They also started to hold European meetings each year in the week after Christmas, in an attempt to sustain the spirituality and communal experience of Taizé. These meetings continue; in December 2011, they were held in Berlin.

1986 Pope John Paul II visit

In 1986, Pope John Paul II visited Taizé and afterwards commented, "One passes through Taizé as one passes though a spring of water" – an image which touched deeply upon the community's longstanding desire that the young people who come to the hillside should be able to drink the living water promised by Christ, and then set out to witness and serve in their own parishes, school, universities and places of work.

The fall of the Berlin Wall

In November 1989, the Berlin Wall came down, and East Germans were permitted to enter West Berlin for the first time since 1961.

Almost overnight Taizé felt the impact of that historic event. The number of visitors reached one hundred thousand that year. The Church of Reconciliation was expanded (again) and several onion domes placed on the roof – a sign of welcome to the thousands of Eastern Orthodox young people visiting Taizé for the first time.

Before the end of 1989 the brothers arranged the European meeting in Poland – the first of its kind in Eastern Europe. It was as if the Community's prayer for reconciliation had begun to be answered.

Settled communal life

In the 1990s, the previously provisional nature of their communal life became more settled, possibly because of the huge numbers who were visiting and possibly too the sign of a community finding a certain maturity, but still passionately living out its charism of solidarity with the poor and welcoming thousands of young people from around the world.

Pilgrimage of Truth on Earth

Trips abroad - far too many to mention - continued. In 1992, the Pilgrimage of Truth on Earth continued in Dayton, Ohio, USA and in the same year George Carey, Archbishop of Canterbury spent a week at Taizé with a thousand young Anglicans.

Pilgrimage of Trust

In 1995, the Pilgrimage of Trust was held in Johannesburg, South Africa, where skyscrapers linked by modern highways contrast starkly with the township houses surrounded by rubbish heaps and evident poverty.

On May 5th, some two thousand young people, most of them black, stayed in some fifty churches in the city – probably the first time they had ever visited these "white" neighbourhoods. This meeting coincided with a growing sense of the need for reconciliation in South Africa, and received a warm message from President Mandela: "I was touched to learn that the bells of Taizé rang out on the day of my liberation from prison".

A tribute to John Paul II

Br. Roger had maintained cordial and regular contact with Pope John Paul II over the years. He had a last private audience with him in March 2004. On the Pope's death in 2005, Br. Roger wrote a moving tribute:

"In his childhood he had lost his mother, and in his youth his father and his only brother. I must try to gladden his heart... by assuring him of the trust our community bore for him. Consumed by love of the Church and of the human family, John Paul II did everything possible to communicate that future. He breathed life into the universality of the church by travelling. He would meet with challenging people and often express great compassion."

Br. Roger stabbed to death

Br. Roger, aged 90, made his last journey in April 2005, to attend Pope John Paul II's funeral in Rome. On August 16th that same year during evening prayer, and in the presence of thousands of young people, a young Romanian woman named Luminiţa Solcan, who was known to be mentally disturbed, stabbed Br. Roger several times with a knife. He died a few moments later.

At the time of his death, many of the brothers were in Cologne, Germany, where about a million young people had gathered for World Youth Day. When news of Br. Roger's death was announced, about fifteen thousand young people, together with numerous church dignitaries, made their way to Taizé, this tiny hill village in Burgundy.

Br. Roger's funeral took place a week later. Cardinal Kasper presided. Br. Alois, the new Prior of Taizé, prayed: "God of goodness, we entrust to your forgiveness,

Luminiţa Solcan, who in an act of sickness put an end to the life of Br. Roger. With trust in the cross we say to you: Father, forgive her, for she does not know what she did." The church was packed and it was raining, but as the funeral ended the clouds blew over and beams of light filled the sky. Br. Roger was with his Creator.

Life continued as normal

Life at Taizé continued as normal, as might be expected in a community which is so imbued with the longing for reconciliation that, even in the face of senseless evil, forgiveness and peace can continue to reside.

Taizé today – a new springtime

Since Br. Roger's death the Community has continued much as before, although several brothers have commented that the pace of community life has increased. If the last ten years of Br. Roger's life had been problematic for some of the community, with many projects "on hold", now it is springtime in the community again and energy flows afresh.

Br. Alois – born in Nördlingen in Bavaria in 1954 – succeeded Br. Roger immediately upon his death. A Catholic, he made his life commitment in the Community in 1978. He continues the work of the founder and the Community continues to flourish.

A passion for love and peace

One writer has said,

> "Although Taizé has in its own right come of age in a post modern world, only time will tell whether or not its passion for love and peace will sustain its appeal for young people in the decades to come. But whatever the future may bring, the brothers of Taizé will continue living faithfully the heart of the gospel of Jesus Christ. They have never judged their own faithfulness by the world's perception of their community's success. Perhaps that is because the brothers understand that God calls all of us to be faithful, not successful."

Visiting Taizé

Welcome to Taizé!

Taizé is off the beaten track. Travel from London is either by train (changing in Paris) to Macon Loché, then a 40 minute bus journey; or from Victoria coach station in one of the special coaches that leave each Saturday around 5.30pm arriving about 8am the following morning. Either way, it is quite a long journey.

On arrival, all young pilgrims are officially welcomed at Casa, Taizé's welcome house. The welcome team then sit you on a wooden bench. The welcomer (a young volunteer) will then explain the routine of Taizé and answer your questions. You are then sent to collect your meal tickets for the week and to make your contribution for lodging (which varies depending on which part of the world you are from). It is a very good deal!

All young pilgrims are asked to undertake a job for the week – it could be the welcome team, the cooking team, food distribution, the clean-up team, working in the Exposition (the gift shop) or Oyak (the snack shop) or bathroom cleaning.

You then deposit your valuables at La Morada (Spanish for "the dwelling"). La Morada also acts as a gateway to the brothers of the Community, where individuals or groups can make an appointment to see a brother.

Accommodation and routine

You either sleep in a Taizé-provided tent (or your own tent) or in one of the barracks - a wooden dormitory sleeping up to six people.

After locating your nearest shower block and cleaning up, dinner is at 7pm. You join a queue of up to five thousand people and enter an ocean of different languages, the most universal being laughter. After a call for silence, a Taizé chant is sung a few times as a "grace" before dinner. You are given a brown tray, a plate, a spoon and a bowl; at Taizé, simplicity is the rule. You will typically receive a hearty ladle of rice, plus a baguette, cream cheese, a piece of fruit, a small packet of biscuits and perhaps a yoghurt. Occasionally meat will be part of the meal.

After dinner, you head for the Church of Reconciliation - the physical centre of the community. Well before "the prayer" (as services are called in Taizé) young people are moving into the cool space in silence (volunteers hold up signs saying "silence" in many languages). You pick up a Taizé song book and enter. While many young people are already sitting on the floor, a few older people are on the benches which line the walls of the church. You find a free spot on the floor and sit down.

You look around. It is probably quite unlike any church you have experienced – it declines gently eastward (cinema style) toward the front. Down the centre is a narrow aisle bordered on each side by artificial hedges, separating the brothers from the visitors. In front of the simple altar are candle filled chimney blocks and behind are long orange sail-like hangings suggestive, perhaps, of the fire of Pentecost. It all creates an atmosphere of stillness, silence, simplicity and beauty. Icons also feature in the church, notably the Virgin and Child, which adorns the Blessed Sacrament altar, along with the Taizé cross which stands to the right, both painted by Br. Eric. This cross might be said to be the symbol of the Community, Copies can be bought at Taizé; in England it is used where there are Taizé services. There are stained glass windows, by Br. Eric, each based on a Biblical theme and in vivid colours.

One by one, the brothers file in, in white albs. They sit in pairs down the centre aisle. As more people filter in, the sound of bells resounds through the church and village summoning everyone to worship, at morning, midday and evening. The bells stop, the church is crowded and the prayer begins.

One of the cantors (a brother) begins a refrain and all join in. (Nothing is announced – all song numbers are displayed on an electronic "scoreboard".) After a few chants, a few verses from Scripture are read in different languages, followed by another song and then a period of silence – usually about 8-10 minutes. Apart from the occasional cough, the church is totally silent and for many of the young pilgrims this is their first real experience of communal silence. The brothers often say that when young people first come it is too long but by the time they leave it is too short! It is here in the silence that they can really face themselves, their lives and relationships, and God, and for many it becomes a positive transformative experience.

Then there is another song, simple prayer of intercession, and then a final song as the Prior, Br. Alois, who sits right at the back of the aisle, gets up and walks out, joined by any younger children who may be there; and then the community follows him from the church. Soon, a brother returns to be available to listen and to speak to the young people.

After this, pockets of young people talk and make their way to Oyak – the only designated "hang-out" area at Taizé. Young people there may buy drinks (one alcoholic drink only per person), chocolate and snacks.

At 11 pm the lights are turned off and all return to tents or dormitories. A night patrol of older long-term volunteers operates through the night to keep good order.

The Daily Routine

7.30am Roman Catholic Mass, in several languages.
8.30am Morning prayer with Holy Communion from the bread and wine consecrated at the 7.30am Mass. Non-

Catholics are invited to receive blessed bread – a custom originating in Eastern Orthodoxy - as a gesture of welcome to all. For many, perhaps most of the young pilgrims, this is their first experience of a daily Eucharist.

Then breakfast – chocolate or coffee, a roll and butter and a piece of chocolate. Then it's time for your Bible Introduction. The young people (as far as possible in language groups) meet with a brother to explore a theme from the Bible, after which they break into smaller groups for discussion prompted by a question sheet given by the brother.

You stay with your small group for the whole week, and sometimes real friendships are made, crossing denominations and national boundaries. The young people experience the passage from different cultural perspectives and learn from each other. It also introduces them to an important part of the communal life at Taizé. You realise that people the world over are struggling with the same, or similar, issues.

12.20pm Midday prayer, then lunch (similar to dinner) at 1pm. Most jobs are carried out in the afternoon, especially picking up litter, a communal activity enjoyed by most.

The brothers prefer pilgrims to remain "on site" for the week but inevitably some make outings to nearby Cluny. Behind the old village of Taizé – with its tiny Romanesque church - Br. Roger and his sister Geneviève are buried in the churchyard, as are some Taizé brothers. Others may choose to walk to La Source – a wooded area with winding paths leading down to a beautiful lake – a place of quiet natural beauty, but often missed by many visitors.

Others make their way to the Exposition (shop) to purchase the brothers' pottery or the many Taizé publications, CDs, and artefacts, including the famous Taizé cross. Sheet music, posters, and post cards are also on sale.

In late afternoon, a series of voluntary workshops are offered, covering a large and varied list of topics; these may include anger management, spirituality through music, understanding icons, being the church in the world, and many more. These are well attended and of a high standard of presentation, complementing the compulsory Bible Introduction.

And then there is supper and evening prayer, as described already. By about Tuesday the routine becomes natural and it begins to feel like (spiritual) "home".

Fridays and Saturdays

The routine on these two days is mostly the same as for Monday to Thursday but on Fridays, Evening Prayer concludes with veneration of the cross. The young people are encouraged to kneel down around the Taizé cross (which is laid flat in the centre of the church) and as on Good Friday, to pray and venerate the cross, and to offer the Lord their sorrows and burdens. This is a most moving part of the liturgy and can take up to an hour. Again, the chants are kept going by several hundred young people who remain long after the conclusion of Evening Prayer.

On Saturdays at Evening Prayer, candles are lit and the church is flooded with the light of Christ. This is a wonderful climax to a week at Taizé and the theme of community is once again emphasised as the light is passed between people. For most, this is another unforgettable experience.

On Sundays, instead of the early Mass, a full Catholic Mass is concelebrated by whatever priests are present and wish to do so.

So Friday to Sunday each week is a re-living of Easter – the integral heart of all Christian life.

Why come to Taizé?

"For over six decades, visitors have called Taizé their spiritual home. Each time they return it's like a homecoming. Why? Much of the mystery of, and attraction to, this unique community stems from the life of Br. Roger, who through a commitment to his own spiritual convictions created a life, and guided a community that ushers in reconciliation to a world in desperate need of peace."

There is no easy answer to this question. But perhaps three themes that could be cultivated and fostered in our churches are reconciliation, freedom and trust.

However, there is no "Taizé theology", Every brother comes from a different tradition (and possibly culture). None is required to break ties with his ecclesiastical tradition; rather, the various numerous traditions are celebrated in their unified fellowship. Each learns from others – if they tried to create a new denomination it would only set them against the most significant aspect of the community, "reconciliation". The acceptance of another Christian ecclesiastical tradition is at the core of what fosters true understanding and forgiveness. "Acceptance is what makes reconciliation in Christ possible."

Reconciliation and acceptance

All humanity is reconciled to God through Christ - so our love for Christ must extend to others by accepting them - especially other Christians. For how can the world know Christ's reconciliation when the church is divided into opposing traditions?

Our differences dissipate when we recognise that Christ is the link in our kinship with other Christians. Christ's death, resurrection, ascension and the Holy Spirit enable us to incarnate Christ's reconciliation to the world. So when we claim Christ's reconciliation as our own, we also accept the calling to become icons of reconciliation: loving our neighbour, because we and our neighbour are loved by Christ. At Taizé this is practised in a very pronounced way. Young people are accepted whatever their background. All are equal in Taizé; the community becomes a living example of reconciliation.

One of Br. Alois's beliefs is that when Christians are truly ready to give their whole lives to the heart of the gospel, the undivided church will merge. True acceptance of our neighbour however is costly. We must focus on what is central to all Christians, and we must acknowledge what is not essential. In accepting others we should concentrate on what unites us.

Many of the young people at Taizé, when questioned about what makes them come back year after year, say simply: "We feel accepted." In Taizé, young people take part in a new way of life in both giving and receiving loving acceptance irrespective of their religious backgrounds, gender, class or ethnicity. But what might this look like in a local church situation?

First, we must look inwards and ask ourselves if we really want to share with others the reconciliation we experience through Christ. We often say it, but are we ready to embrace the gospel and its care for the poor and needy? Are we willing to worship among different traditions or ethnic groups, or is our call for diversity only lip service? In other words, do we really want to accept others who are not the same as us? For when Christ made all things new, he restored us in the image of God – and this was restored in all humanity. As a consequence when we see our neighbour, we ought to see the image of God – we ought to see Christ. And we may have to take risks (as Christ willing accepted the path to the cross) making ourselves vulnerable and open to rejection.

Secondly, we must not view our own tradition as exclusive and we must see God at work in all of them. At Taizé, denominational traditions are not forgotten, but there is more emphasis on the common Christian gospel. We must meet, get to know, and come to love each other. All local churches need to see this as a priority if we are to share the Good News of Christ with others. But do we?

Finally, we need to look for all kinds of ecumenical opportunities between our churches.

Freedom and Peace

Despite the basic rules, pilgrims to Taizé do not usually feel constrained – in fact although they are expected to worship three times a day, do a work task, and take part in a Bible introduction group, many claim that they experience a freedom that they have never felt before. They enjoy the activities. No one is monitoring them or checking up on them. Amazingly, very few skip prayer or Bible introduction. There are, of course, some, boundaries, for instance those involving alcohol and Oyak, and everyone is expected to be in bed by 11.30pm. These freedoms mirror the Rule of the Community, the essence of which seeks only to delineate "the minimum necessary for a community to build itself in Christ, and give itself up to a common service of God." (Rule of Taizé).

The young people of Taizé are also free from – no longer bound by – the ecclesial or societal structures that seem to oppress them. In the words of one 26 year old: "Here I am free. Taizé is a kind of utopia for me." Or another "In Taizé we are free not to hate. It doesn't exist here… it's a paradise on Earth." Many of the young people link this sense of freedom with the prayers.

When you enter the Church of Reconciliation, you experience freedom and peace. The vast space is free for people to sit in, people are free to sing or to listen, during the silence nothing is imposed upon the visitors. At

Taizé, all are invited, all are free to experience the holy, to encounter the sacred and to meet the living God.

Do we offer our young people freedom from the pressures of the world? Are there sacred times and places in our churches where young people can escape the media-saturated, consumer-driven, marketing society? Or do we offer them merely another version of what the world offers them?

Over a hundred thousand young people come to Taizé every year – hardly for the music alone, but for the sense of freedom and peace they find in a community defined by reconciliation and acceptance.

Trust

Many of those who come to Taizé from around the world are seeking something greater than they are finding in our churches. What they find is an ecumenical community that genuinely trusts them enough to share in the communal work of a life together. They all have a job (given not chosen!) and they are trusted to get on with it and they do. At Taizé, trust is given, not earned. They are given responsibility – and are serving both Christ and one another at the same time.

While the prayers connect them to God, the work connects them to each other. Many young people report that they really feel part of the community through their work tasks. They are needed, valued, trusted. Do we trust them in their home churches?

After Br. Roger's murder in 2005, the brothers' trust in their visitors was even more remarkable and noticeable. No barricades were erected and no security measures taken to ensure the safety of the community. The brothers believe this is part of their calling in life – to trust those they have no reason to trust – just as God relates to us. Because of our sinful inclinations, this brings risks. But the trust that is exhibited is in the end all the more powerful.

Perhaps more than simply importing the chants, we need to import these other powerful aspects of Taizé - reconciliation, freedom and trust – if our young people are to grow into the likeness of Christ and so transform their world and themselves in the process.

Four secrets of Taizé

1. Young people respond to warmth and affection. Hypocrisy they spot immediately. Age is irrelevant (many, although not all, of the Taizé brothers are considerably older than the 17-35 year old age group who come). Love is the key quality which encourages young people to trust and value any person. The relations at Taizé, both between the young and the brothers, and between the young themselves, demonstrate this.

2. Valuing the qualities which young adults can bring to church life. Social convention often disguises the feelings of older people but the young are refreshingly honest, open and revealing. They are not embarrassed to ask questions about religion – what does it mean? Why do we do this or that?

3. Participation: young people hate being spectators – they want to be involved! At Taizé there is plenty of opportunity from peeling potatoes to leading a discussion group and much else besides. And because they are involved, they feel valued. At the prayers, too, they are not put off by silence or contemplation. Their powers of concentration and their desire to experience God are not inferior to those of older people.

4. The young respond to genuine spirituality. Many ask questions about the meaning and purpose of life and they react positively to adults who treat them as intelligent and developing people. Taizé's experience of working with young people confirms this.

The Sacraments at Taizé

The Eucharist

For Catholics, the Mass (the Eucharist) is the centre of worship and it might be thought that this would be an insuperable barrier in an ecumenical setting such as Taizé. The brothers have struggled with this over the years and have sought a solution which preserves the central prominence of the Eucharist, and yet which respects the conscience of all who may visit the community.

Each morning, Monday to Saturday, a Catholic Mass is celebrated at the back of the Church of Reconciliation, in one of the sectioned-off areas. This is a concelebration, and any Catholic priest present (either Community member or visitor) is invited to concelebrate. I have taken part in this on many occasions, and it is a joy to concelebrate with priests from around the world - each in his own language, for the liturgy including the Eucharistic prayer is multi-lingual. There can be as many as twenty-five priests concelebrating.

The early morning Mass, at 7.30am, can attract up to three hundred young Catholics (although non-Catholics attend from time to time.) It is a moving experience and brings home very well the catholicity (universality) of the church. The liturgy includes a few Taizé chants.

At the end of Mass, the remaining consecrated elements are taken solemnly in procession to the foot of the Church of Reconciliation and reverently reserved in a large tabernacle on a side altar.

Slowly, the main church begins to be filled with the young people, who can number up to five thousand at the height of summer. Towards the end of morning prayer, an announcement is made:

"Holy Communion will now be distributed from the bread and wine consecrated at the Catholic Mass earlier this morning."

All the brothers of the Community take up position around the church to administer communion.

It is made clear that non-Catholics may receive the blessed bread which is also available at various points. Young Protestant communicants may receive from another administration point.

This arrangement is of course not ideal and does not stop the community from working toward that day when all Christians are in communion with each other and when the Eucharist can be completely shared.

It is worth making a few additional points:

• It works. Thousands of people receive communion in about ten minutes reverently without hurry or fluster - most parishes take that long - and no one feels excluded.

• Communion is administered to the whole community of brothers, many of whom are not Catholics but who completely understand and accept Catholic teaching on this matter – one of the absolutely central requirements of an ecumenical community. This is done with the permission of the local Bishop.

• For the vast majority, even of practising young Catholics, this is their first real experience of daily communion – an experience that will remain with them. The atmosphere is highly spiritual and reverent,.

• At the end, the elements are carefully covered, and all the remaining hosts are reserved by a small team of brothers.

• The Orthodox Liturgy is also celebrated periodically - for example, when an Orthodox priest is visiting.

• On Sundays a full Catholic Mass is celebrated for the whole community. Occasionally the local Bishop presides. All the priests present concelebrate.

The Sacrament of Reconciliation

Daily provision is made for Catholics to make their confession. At the end of Evening Prayer, seven or eight priests (representing a spread of languages and identified by wearing a purple stole) stand along one side of the church, while a few of the brothers stand on the other side. This way, people can choose whom to approach.

Both the sacrament and the confidential talk with a brother are very informal and are surely a great means of good, allowing the young people open their hearts and lives.

During this, many more are still in the centre of the church singing. All of this can go on until very late. The church is never closed.

Taizé and Rome

The story of Taizé is inextricably bound up with the eventual goal of the union of all Christians, respecting the ministry of the Bishop of Rome as universal pastor.

The relationship between Taizé and the Vatican has been a thread running through the life of the Community, from Br. Roger's first meeting with Pope Pius XII in 1950, and the seminal meeting with Pope John XXIII in 1958 to his attendance at the funeral of Pope John Paul II in April 2005.

The first meeting with Pope John XXIII just a few days after his election was a crucial turning point in Br. Roger's life, in the Taizé community, and in the ecumenical movement. Let Br. Roger speak for himself:

> "From our first meeting, we had the certainty that we were loved, understood. John XXIII left an indelible mark on us... Through him, springtime entered our community. It was like a new beginning for us.
>
> John XXIII remains the man I have revered the most on Earth. I loved him like a father. Through his life, we grasped what the ministry of a universal pastor meant.
>
> At our last meeting, shortly before he died, he told us: "The Catholic Church is made up of circles that are always larger, larger, larger."

He didn't say exactly in which circle he saw us, but we understood that, for him, we were within these circles... His words inserted us, as it were, within the reality of the Church."

After John XXIII died in 1963, Br. Roger was received every year by the Pope at a private audience.

A reflection

I have been to Taizé many times with young people from schools, universities, and parishes. Each visit provides new reflections about this remarkable monastic Community and its even more remarkable founder.

As I walk past the walls and the complex of houses in which the brothers live, I reflect that behind those walls live up to a hundred men who, in order to be together, have had to clear many historical hurdles. First, in the early years, there was the scepticism and outright opposition of many in the Protestant world to such a way of life, hitherto only associated with Catholicism. Then, the almost unbridgeable gap of four hundred years separating Catholics and Protestants; together with the obstacles separating the different Protestant denominations to whom the brothers belong. And, on top of that, the issues that have estranged the western churches in particular from exploited, oppressed young people.

It is remarkable that the family of celibate men has been able to create bonds with, and among, all of these categories of people; and they have been able to do so because they have taken all the above mentioned barriers into their own home. About a hundred brothers of different ethnicity, nationality, age, denomination and political leaning, are yet all a part of the same family who share what they have, spiritually as well as materially.

I will end with a quotation from a book on Taizé published in 1978 which sums up, I believe, the Taizé Community and its founder, Br. Roger.

"Taizé has lit a clearly visible candle. Its light shines in the Church where it moves beyond criticism to illuminate new inspirations which sooner or later will lead to a rebirth. It shines in the world, too, where Taizé orients itself towards the sick and the needy, the oppressed and the lonely, because it knows that through them Christ speaks to us. Its light shines personally on all of Taizé's many visitors, the tens of thousands of young people especially who lay their problems at the brothers' and each other's feet. They fix their attention above all on the light within each one of them, the light they can either extinguish or fan into flame. Each of them, says Taizé, can be a sign of hope. Together we can invent the world.

"The embodiment of that hope is a small, greying man whose smile has a touch of sadness in it... out of his hope, his trust, and love has come into being a movement within the church which can only be compared with the new life that a Benedict or a Francis gave to the Church.

"In the place where young Roger Schutz, all alone, dug up the hard earth, communion is being shared; where he healed the wounds of refugees, and where he descended in contemplation into the solitude of his heart, there now blossoms the prayers of people who come from the far corners of the Earth.

This place has captured my heart."

Amen to that.